# Peace Begins When
# Family Violence Ends

# Peace Begins When Family Violence Ends

*Chelsea Elizabeth Greene*

InspiringVoices®

Inspiring Voices books may be ordered through booksellers or by contacting:

Inspiring Voices
1663 Liberty Drive
Bloomington, IN 47403
www.inspiringvoices.com
1 (866) 697-5313

Because of the dynamic nature of the Internet, any web addresses or links contained in this book may have changed since publication and may no longer be valid. The views expressed in this work are solely those of the author and do not necessarily reflect the views of the publisher, and the publisher hereby disclaims any responsibility for them.

Certain stock imagery © Thinkstock.
Any people depicted in stock imagery provided by Thinkstock are models,
and such images are being used for illustrative purposes only.

ISBN: 978-1-4624-1029-3 (e)
ISBN: 978-1-4624-1028-6 (sc)

Library of Congress Control Number: 2014913597

Printed in the United States of America.

Inspiring Voices rev. date: 9/18/2014

# Dedication

To my son –
Whom I am so thankful for and so very proud of…
I dedicate this book to you and your future.

I am a very happy mother – we share a special bond, a family connection that
no matter where in the world we may be, we are always connected.

Thank you for all the wonderful memories – the challenges and the good times we remember.
You helped motivate me to take action, to dream and to stay grounded – when I had to
take risks, you encouraged me, and taught me how to have better boundaries. Your will
and inner strength when times were tougher than nails gave me courage to take risks.

I will continue to grow, learn, and "Be the Peace" because you are my child and I am your mother.

# Professional Comments

Chelsea provided professional counseling in our medical pediatric office in a rural community. Her work has included family advocacy, human services, child welfare, and professional counseling. She has been an advocate for family and domestic violence education and prevention. This book *Peace Begins*, is a motivation and inspirational true story to help families and children.
Dr. Masoud Ahdieh, MD

You have widened my sense of what is possible ... as you write about the struggle for psychic survival, your words can help me to dare to try and express deeper issues in my life,may you grow in wisdom and love for many, many years to come.
Dr. Tony Pearce,PHD
Norwich University

As a therapist, Chelsea has always had the client as a priority; she has used solid clinical judgement, this book is about the art of the creative process... and its therapeutic value for families and children who are dealing with family violence,healing and recovery.
Dr. Joseph Apollo, Ph.D art of creative healing

Chelsea has transformed an amorphous view of wholeness and healing into a new view of creative and transformational wholeness. She has worked her way thru a great deal of inner defenses and pain to a place or greater freedom. This poetic story of healing will inspire others.
Dr. James Farr, Ph.D

# Acknowledgements

I thank God for his grace.

I thank the folks at Guidepost, Inspiring Voices, that I know and don't know that participated in making this book a reality. Thank you for your expertise, excellence and for providing me a platform to publish, for helping me share the message to *end all forms of family violence and hold the sacred space for peace to begin.* Poetry is medicine for the soul, publishing and marketing it to help other men, women and children a larger task – Thank You!

I want to thank Joyce Blackley of Blackley's Printing & Sign Shop in Clayton, North Carolina and Joyce's staff, for being so focused and encouraging. They have provided typing, and editing assistance. Joyce, thank you for your encouraging words, "the world is open to you."

Thanks to Amy Ammons Garza, my writing coach and teacher, founder/writer of "Catch the Spirit of the Appalachia," you told me I am a writer and poet… I didn't believe you, but you helped shape my destiny; and gave me encouragement to "pick up my pen."

Thanks for the support and therapeutic relationships I had with Dr. James Farr, Ph.D., founder of Farr Associates in Greensboro, NC, Dr. Ginny Wright, Ph. D, Dr. Steven DeBerry, and many others who supported me in my own "healing space" during the "healing years" of my life.

Thank you to significant others, my son, my mother, brothers, my former husbands Bob and Tony and other family members. In addition to Eliel Pierre, writer, friends- Pat, Rick, Ruth, Karen and Dave, Pastor Ben, Steve, Randy, Grace Church, Chuck, Linda, Judy & Mike in Waynesville, NC whose house on top of the mountains in which I lived and where I wrote many of the "story poems". Also, my legal friends John, George and Chris.

# Introduction

This "true story" and table top poetry book has been written during the last 10 years from 2004 – 2014. It reflects a life story – of events – and the experience of healing from family violence. It was during the "healing years" of my life, that I started this collection of poems. I never imagined it would become a book that could help many other people – men, women and children – resolve to stop all forms for family violence and let peace begin.

I wrote most of these poems living on top of a mountain on the Blue Ridge Parkway, alone by myself for nine months – it was during those nine months, I pieced myself back together, integrated years of therapy and made a decision to dedicate my life to helping others heal and restore their own lives from the wounds of family and domestic violence. Knowing this would not be easy topics to talk about nor to heal from and change, it seemed that my journey in life had lead me to the "top of the mountain" to begin that process. I wrote my truth, my experience and did my best to invite healing and peace into the dark places where the light was very dim.

As a licensed professional counselor, I hold a Master's Degree in Counseling Psychology and from 25 years of experience and combined education, I know people can heal from all forms of domestic/family violence. It can end, and peace can begin for future generations of children and families.

Peace Begins™ – a Family Violence 12 Step Recovery Program – has been birthed from the completion of this story, narrative and healing poetry book.

If you want more information about the Peace Begins: Family Violence Recovery Program, please visit www.SageofNC.com.

# Borrowed Heritage

# I AM THE STORY

Because, I am the child.
I am the story,
And, I can't just forget,
As I pass your way.

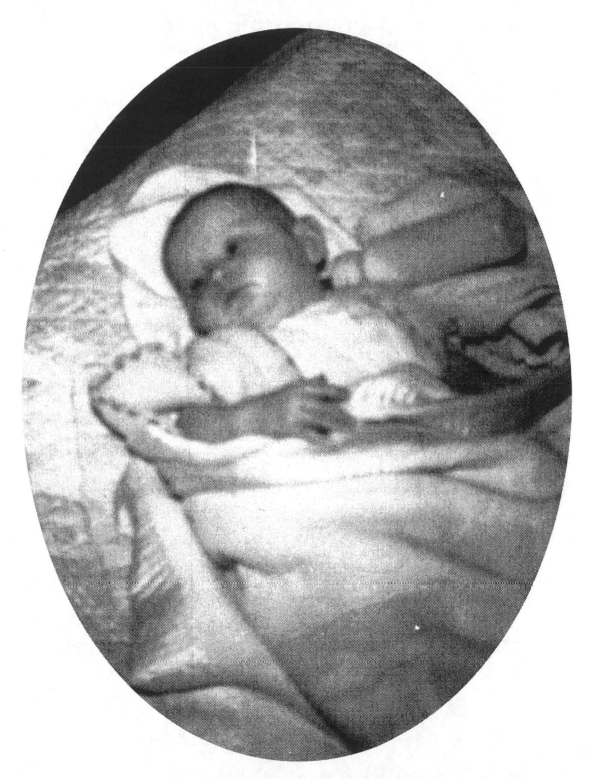

# BORROWED HERITAGE

My heritage is borrowed from you.
You may not know me,
But I am your sister, your brother, mother and father.
Every child, I see.

Kinship from this human race, we are connected by history and by our bond of God's love.

God's love, it weaves us together in different ways,
the Miracle of heritage that we share.

We may have a different religion,
But we share God's love which bonds us into our heritage as Soul.

Your eyes, carry your soul,
Your ears, they can hear,
Listen to the sound of this God's love and
See the light as it brightens your way back home.

We share a common bond,
One that can heal all of our wounds.

The circle of life, common to you and me,
Making miracles and memories,
Magic and madness,
It's more than you and
It's more than myself,
It's our Borrowed Heritage.

# ONLY SOUL KNOWS

Only soul can see the wind and
Know it is God painting on your eyelashes.

Only soul knows the design
That can never be grasped
By the edges of the mind.

Only soul realizes,
God lives in a kingdom inside.

So, go ahead, and
Lie down beside still waters.

And, rest,
For soul, will still be there
Even when the waters of life don't flow.

Only soul sings when the warrior gathers,
A chorus to make you stronger.

Soul plays in a sea of letting go,
Of forgetfulness and
Making the worst of garbage smells,
Into a piece of framed Mozart.

Only soul sees the wind and
Knows God has painted on your baby eyelashes.

# MOTHER CLEO, FATHER JAMES

You must have met when the world was kind,
The pictures tell me so.

Park benches, beach picnics, and your clothes so brand new.

Smiles, young love simply touches Mother Cleo and Father James.

What happened? When you went to sleep?
Did your love fall to sleep?
Why did it all fall apart?
You lost your love and the dream woke up.

So, just like that,
The curtain of darkness drapes descending over your love,
Interrupted by lust, lost in a lingering love dust.

Mother Cleo,
Father James,
You're forgiven and you're both free,
You're full-and further along now.

So go ahead,
And love yourself a sea of love memories

# ABANDONED

Mother leaves so quickly,
And soon I forget.

Snowy day all so pure and all so white,
And the sun glistening in the perfect scene
as I await, abandonment.

Packed up the car, she waved goodbye,
Placed in the stroller,
Behind the fenced-in gate,
I was left, on the sidewalk.

Wiping her tears, all alone.

Tenderness without tears,
I sat, a little one, watching as still as death.

Snow falling, spaces in between,
snowflakes so cold,
so bitter and mean.

Abandoned and remembering
her waving goodbye.

Passing cars never noticed,
the bundle of joy
wondering at the world.

Snow falling and wind blowing,
on a quiet afternoon.

Cold winds blow and the wheels began to roll,
Stroller geared in reverse, rolling back and forth
Time stopping at the gate.

Cold baby hands,
Cold feet and tiny toes,
Crying in fear, crying out for mother,
the baby without comfort.

Mother with hope,
Two souls dancing in agreement,
Abandoned, just like that.

Remember hearing people talking,
Nobody could see,
The stroller wheels against the gate.

And then she came,
My Nanny came.
She wept away the snow-capped tears.
And, she began to kiss my fingertips.

# NANNY GREENE

She was my Nanny Greene,
And I was her Grand Daughter Child.
Regal, royal, and right about me.

She was strong,
And so was I.

She was soft,
And, so was I.

She came from heaven,
And, so did I.

She never looked back when she left.

Through the door to walkway.

Waiting for the bus,
Saving her coins to catch the afternoon bus.

Button up her cashmere coat,
Favorite hat and purse held inside her elbow bend.

She was my Nanny Greene,
Skin softer than angel dust,
Drinking black coffee in the middle of the night
Laughing with Ed Sullivan.

She'd stand up, shut up, firm
And, tell him to sit down and shut up, too.

She'd worry where he was at night.

She'd hold me and when the house shook,
she held me on her lap and
Whispered a never-be-afraid song in my ear.

# GRANDMA SMITH

She was sweet,
Tender a drop of morning dew,
A yellow buttercup connected to the earth.

Her heart knew no evil way, Bathed in the morning glory,
Stray dogs found their way to her front door.

Love filled her heart,
Sitting on the front step
Watching as we children played.

Grandma Smith.
We all know her.
She dreamed secrets and heartfelt ways.

Iron those shirts,
Smiles from the corner of her mouth
Pick-up sticks and sweep the dust away.

Fold the white linen clothes,
Fry chicken livers,
And snap green peas,
Button up for warmth on cold days.

Grandma Smith could see inside of you,
She had eyes behind her head.
Laughter and jokes, she said,
"Now go play."

# MISS GIBSON

Miss Gibson was a favorite memory.

Loving me as a child,
Fleeing to her from the storm,
Daddy fighting in the living room.

Big house on the corner,
Porch light swarmed with lightning bugs.
Run on over, she would say,
Don't stay and watch the fight.

Come sit with me, baby girl.

Miss Gibson, please hug me real tight.
Sit down at the kitchen table,
Red plastic chair pads,
Table legs of steel.

Miss Gibson would feed me love
And cookies dipped in hopefulness.

Here hair bucked up inside the brown hair net,
Her robe with silver snap buttons,
Bedroom slippers from Murphy's dime store down on Decatur Street.

Flat and dirty, the cracks on her foot healing,
Inviting me to crawl way up inside her yellow flowered night gown.
Never walking back across Decatur Street
Just to watch them fight some more.

Oh, how I loved Miss Gibson.
My favorite memory,
Always there in the midnight hours.
Thankful Porch Light,
Shining Bright,
Just for me.

# AUNT DOT

She watched her brother fall into the gutter,
Drunken, homeless, and weak with lovelessness...
No leg to stand on.

She talked about how he was full of nothing,
As she decorated her little girl, and
Roped off the living room like a museum.
Plastic covers on the sofa,
Chairs red velvet Victorian,
Room for viewing.

Wait your turn at Christmas,
Stand still and look at Brenda's presents.
Tissue paper and boxes
Saved from last year

She was Aunt Dot,
Father's drowning sister woman,
Empty crystal glass vases,
Tarnished silver and old candy in a dish.
Perfect paintings of the
Little Blue Boy and the
Little Pink Girl.

So, go throw up outside her back door,
'Cause Daddy's favorite suit
Smells like Jack Daniels,
And the old green Plymouth ran out of gas.

No food, No money,
Let's go see Aunt Dot.
She's in the hospital.

Bound down in her chair,
Hair cold and black,
Skin pale white,
With no legs to stand.

Let's go give her a hand.

# ROOTS OF REJECTION

Roots of Rejection,
Make it so hard to know love.

Roots of Rejection,
Mama said goodbye and walked away.

All because she knew no other way.

Bruised and broken and battered,
Wonder if she'll heal her Roots of Rejection.

In some kinder way, Roots of Rejection
Swept up Daddy's broken bottle of beer.

Sad, heartless, monster of fear
No glory until the very end.

Roots of Rejection,
Buried while alive
Coiled around the heart,
Tying us together.

Grown up and mightily
Swords of redemption,
Cut you loose.

Healed, and broken memory stand triumph,
Strong and still,
Breath of wonder,
The warrior child within.
Redeemed from the Roots of Rejection,
Intergenerational healing begins.

# TWO BROTHERS AND ME

Two brothers,
And, neither one knows
Who's my Daddy?
And, where did Mama go?

Two brothers, one just a half,
Stayed with Mother.
And, brother and me,
We were left.

That's me, and the sister who appeared,
Disappeared, yesterday gone, no memory.
And she, then us,
Me, lost in between two brothers.

Chaos in the center of the world,
Trusting nobody,
Close no more.

Then violence,
Tears swept down the stairs,
Running away from the fire,
Brother left on the floor.

Hearing the gun shots,
Get me out fast,
Run, two brothers.

One day change comes,
And the sun did rise to shine.

I called, Brother, Where's Mama?
And, who's my Daddy?

The harsh wind blowing,
The scarf from Mama's head left behind,
Rocks covered with snow top,
No bread for tiny birds.

Mama gone,
Somebody's children got left behind.

Two brothers, holding my hand,
And I stand knowing,
Pretending to be a swinging bridge,
And, I am the roaring river.

# NO FOOD, NO SHELTER

No food, no shelter when he was thrown out late at night.
Down beside the corner A & P store parking lot
Lay his head under the bush,
Gravel stones in his ears.
Wake up to remember the children are.

Lost in alcoholic night sweats, dreams,
Still a child himself
And all alone.

No more Mama,
No more Daddy,
Comfort all gone.

How am I going to talk to the children
When they get all grown up and
I am nowhere to be found?

No food, no shelter wondering when the sun will ever shine.

Back in the war,
At least we laughed and played checkers
Watched the women,
And wondered how we got to be grown men.

No food, no shelter,
And here I am now,
Two little ones,
And my hands are not free.

Tied up in the memories of yesterday,
Please fix me, God.

No more guns,
And no more wars,
It has not made me free.

No food, no shelter,
And, I have come home to give my children food and shelter.

# HOLD ON TO YOUR INNOCENCE

She cried out and nobody heard.
She wondered if they were all the same…

Liars, cheaters, violence filled, animals
Lost in a place they called love,
She knew nothing of peace,
so, she went deep inside.

And, a voice told her to
Hold On to Your Innocence.

They told her the world was full of sin,
And, her sin was the worst of all.

Her heart could not bloom, in guilt and grief,
She knew nothing of peace,
So she went deep inside,

And, a voice told her to
Hold On to Your Innocence.

They spoke untruths and blame,
She could never make it all up.

She knew her lost innocence lived
In the water cells of her being.

She knew nothing of peace,
Yet in her heart,
She heard a deep inside melody.

Holding onto her innocence with dear life.

# HOW CAN I GROW UP?

How can I grow up,
When I am already so old?

Solving problems of hurt and fear,
Watching the thunder storms
In the living room and
Over the dining room table.

Fights and fear,
Problems for me to solve.
How can I grow up,
When I am already so old.

Little child in a
Great big soul.
Wounded creation of genius.
How can I grow up when I am already so old?

Little small one remembers to stare into the camera,
Tilting her head in amazement,
Watching through eyes of tunnels,
Holding on to original remembrance...

Knowing she had become all grown up.

She would return as a little child.

# VULNERABLE CHILD

Vulnerable child,
Left without protection.

No power,
And nobody knows who you are,
A small daisy flower
Innocent and free.

Left to be without your mother,
Father is never home.

The whole world stands still,
And a kiss from the invisible
Makes a mark on you
Surrounding you, forever with dignity
No matter how dark life can be.

How do I start and end today?
Nobody knows, I just want to play.
As a vulnerable child, laugh, don't cry
Alone.

You can never know why,
or fill up the void,
Yet in a single moment
You can make a difference that frees.

Oh, little child found sitting all alone,
with the daisy and the tree.

# MEMORIES SPEAK

Memories speak tells me about the days when I was young,
Too much to bear upon the shoulders of a little one.

Memories speak to pictures of those days…
Violent, loud, angry, drunken man, lonely,
Lost, beaten woman statue.

Memories speak children pretending not to exist.
Please, God.
Hold my Hand.

Keep me safe in the night.
Kitchen knives in the drawer,
Leather belt, or
Just his hand…
His tight fist.

Memories speak…
I will pretend.
Line up all my stuffed animals.
Tell them my speech.
Pretend to be the teacher.
Use the TV antennae as a microphone.

Set the stage – Lights, Action, Bondage – soon to be free.

Memories speak…
Say what it was like,
A child living in family violence,
Abuse and neglect, abandonment, no one free.

Alone – no one to see.

# Family Violence and the Voice of the Child

# THE VOICE

Let me Speak,
It's my turn.

And, I will tell you the story,
Like it was very long ago.

I will tell you how it really happened.
I will tell you the gospel truth about
How they lived in vain,
How they cut the hearts of children
Into tiny pieces
And turned their tiny fingerprints into
Memories of black ink.

Of the purest pain,
Let me speak.
Footprints traveling on journeys of
Unsung glory.

I am the child, Forgotten.

With abuse...
My heritage,
Hero unsung.

I now sing
Because I am the hero!

So, sister,
As I speak,
Let me tell the story,
Once and for all.

I remember hiding in the closet,
Behind the bathroom door,
And clutched behind the seat in the car,
Speeding...

Hearing the tires screech,
Drunken mad man,
Father, nobody,
No soul.

Mad at the world,
Crashing in the wall.

I remember playing prayer
Behind the trash cans.
No food,
Pretending not to exist here,
but somewhere near the Heart of God
Hidden in the Kingdom.

I am the child,
Let me tell you the story.
So, if you see yourself,
Forget to feel.

Send in a helping hand in the darkness
If you see this next door.

Nobody knew me.
Nobody cared.
Small little child.
Walking into the State Jail.

Father behind jail bars.
Bottles, clanging,
Hitting the walk way.

Sorrow lasting forever,
Hollow hearts without a pulse,
Mother pass the blood alcohol,
Drained away so I could live.

Infant graves,
Into the child.

Listen before you speak;
And, remember my story.

Chased down by ghost of haunting dreams,
Never safe,
Never secure,
No blanket to keep me warm.

Late to play, late to eat, late to be loved,
One more birthday, just another day
Before I am all grown up.

Left Mother, Father, Brothers, too.
Left with my story.
Safe, but trembling as it may.

Tremble as the earth quakes.
Silence in the night, and
I knew what I know.

# GONE, GONE, WHERE DID THEY GO?

Everybody's gone.
Can't remember why.
Just know they are never coming back.

Left me here in the little green house.
Decatur Street,
Buddy Dale Hat Shop and
The A & P Store parking lot.

Beer joints lining up Hull Street,
I'm swinging in the porch glider now.

Gone, gone, and
I am told to find them.
Six-year-old girl,
Walking into stinky, smelly beer joints.

Looking for who?
Oh, they left yesterday.

Makes me dizzy,
My head turns round and round.
Passing out on the sidewalk.

Please get me out of here.

# IF PAIN

If pain is all I remember,
How can I know joyful-You?

I wonder,
I look at the stars, I talk to the Father Robin who greets me at the door,
Early afternoon,
Then you touch me,
And, I forget.

Forget all my pain,
And I remember.

Joy.

Joy you can never forget.
If pain is free,
If pain never came,
How would we know Love.

Love,
The pulse inside of joyful?

# HOUSE OF FIRE

When he came home, plumbing pipes broke,
She was lying down with another, Mother.

Children playing in the dirt,
Lunch left over on the kitchen sink,
Loud TV with turning knobs,
Watching an old TV show.

He went mad, Father
And pulled out his gun.
Run to the closet and hide,
Big brother,
We can't play, run away.

House of fire,
Going up in flames.
Burning his memories.

Call to the police for help.
House of fire,
It is too late.
Nothing in the rooms no more,
Empty shelves and
Plain hard wood floors.

Climb the stairs and windows torn.
Where did she go when he came home?

Running away,
Far from home.
Children drinking milk.
Watching as he wondered.

House of Fire,
Wind blowing through,
Whirling round and round,
As ashes land, on butterflies' wings.

# THE BELT

The Belt was his weapon against his children.
Children better be still,
Eat and only listen.
Fear the pain.

I am in control.
You are little
And, I am big.

Watch the belt as it hits the skin,
Brother, stepmother.
And, now off I go to the State Pen.

The belt,
A weapon of fear.
I laid it on the floor,
Over the chair,
And when I needed control,
It walked.

Slapped me down once,
And I could not get back up.
So I crawled under the bed until I woke up
With dust in my nose and tears in my eyes.

You wear that belt
And remember where it put you
The State Pen, praise and Amen.

Stepmother lived, brother played again,
And nobody's crawling under the bed no more.

# RAGE

He was horrible, never friendly or kind,
Angry all the time.

Playing only twice that I recall,
The trip to Washington and to
Buck Roe Beach.

Always raging,
Planting seeds of rage that
Covered the heart with a
Cast iron skillet.

The rage was always at the alcohol,
And no money.
Not a day of peace.
Clutching at kitchen table,
Drinking his tears as they fell into his skillet.

Kitchen chair, kids, kitchen wall.
Telephone pulled of the wall.
Stewing in his cigarette smoke.

Little girl thrown upside the
Refrigerator door.
No money for food.

Stop asking, Can I eat?
Desperate days of rage.
So sorry,
So sorry.

Pull the curtains.
Lock the doors.
When he leaves, pray he will never return.

Watch TV,
Wonder what will happen next.
Rage, black and blue eyes.
Mother Erma all beat up.

Lying on the kitchen floor,
Frozen in fear,
Get up,
Pour him a glass of water.

Stay quiet,
Sleep under the bed,
Way up in the corner.

Dusty floor with no pillow.
Falling asleep and
Waking up in fear.
Sun never shining.

Rage,
he never felt love.
Couldn't control himself,
He became the mark of the beast.

A beast,
A bad, bad man.

My Father,
Rage.

# WHISPERS IN MY EAR

Whisper,
So he won't hear.

She'd tell me when he'd come home.
"Never be afraid," in my ear.
Whisper to your brother when you play.
He's hungry,
And been gone for a week long drunk.

Not sure when he left or
When he decided to return.
But, remember to whisper if he comes in, and
"Never be afraid," in my ear.

She'd leave for work, and
We would wait.
Remembering if he comes home,
To whisper, be still.

Maybe he'll sleep…
And, never be afraid.

Open the window, and
Peek outside.
Watch to see if he walks across
The A & P parking lot.

Whisper, Whisper,
Be real quiet.
We all know what he does when he gets mad.

Whisper,
Don't weep…and,
"Never be afraid."

# BEHIND CLOSED DOORS

He walked in and
Shut the door.

It was quick,
And he was done.

Left in the dark,
And, alone.

Terrified,
Feeling my heart beat until I ceased.

Numb and full of rage.
Fall asleep and forget,
Morning will never come.

Wet and slippery cold.
Full and frozen, he's getting old.
Breathless child.

Behind closed doors,
And, she remembers.

Silent night,
Holy night.
No more.

He made it clear as he said,
If you tell…

I wished I would have
locked the door.
Promises, Promises.

Disappearing darkness
Without the light.

Behind closed doors
Pretending to be a teacher.

Dressed up all pretty,
Toy animals and stuffed teddy bears
Learning the lessons from the night.
Disassociation, wounded,
In the night.

# MEAN MAN

Mean man run away from me,
Go and never come back.

I pray every day,
And pray every night,
That the mean man will go away.

Mean man hates in his heart,
Cold and lonely
Deep dark blue.

Mean man,
Who do you know,
Turned inside and
Only a mean man?

Mean man,
Bitter and full of harmfulness.
Broken spirit and end the violence,
whole world wide, families free.
Now teach your boy,
Children, how not to be.

Mean man,
When I watch you walk away,
I imagine you will disappear.
Captured by the tree limbs,
Where you sit and hold your head to cry.

Mean man, I used to tell my teacher, who was a man.

I call Daddy, Mean Man,
Mean enough to break my heart and soul
Into a thousand and one pieces.

And, the teacher said, "Mean man doesn't mean to be so mean.
Maybe one day you will see the mean man in a different way."

# DRINKING MONEY

Drinking money is always black.

It coils itself inside the pockets of holes.

Out again and spending drinking money,
Should have put food in the bottom of the basement.

Drinking money is always black.

It lies and steals.
It never tells the truth.

Drinking money takes all the fun from the little children.

Drinking money,
Work all day,
Empty pockets,
Wondering in the mirror
where your smile has retracted to.

Drinking money,
Madness without any meaning.

Far from the shopping stores,
And, never on a fancy trip.
Just floating on a dime,
Down a stream of worthlessness.

Drinking money pays you back,
When nobody cares where you have been.
So go on and spend your life on
Drinking money.

# THE ATTACK ON DADDY

We decided he had to die.
Little kids building the fort from
Tall broken pine trees,
Horses in the pasture.

We decided he had to die,
Sing hallelujah and
Watch the angels fly.

Make up a plan and get ready,
Daddy's gonna die.

When he comes through the door,
You and I hide.
Brother, me on each side, door opens wide, he staggers in,
Fire stick and lamp,
Daddy's gonna die.

Hit as hard as you can,
Knock him down and run.

Run for our life and
Never look back.

Run down the highway,
Brother, left crying and all alone.

Run in the dark,
Scream in the night.

*Peace Begins When Family Violence Ends*

Ten years old,
Ten years flash, bye
In the night.

Help,
Can anyone see,
Daddy's gonna die,
Because of me.

Help, said the Policeman,
Where can the children go?
Daddy's back at home, and
I am so sad.

Little children run into the fort,
Watch the horses play,
And listen to the angels sing.

# HIGHWAY LINES

You have a right,
You deserve the best,
Stand up and protect yourself.
If you don't they will take your soul,
Defend yourself.

Keep your stride and follow
The lines on the highway.
Do whatever it takes to keep to the
Straight path.
Defend yourself.

Nothing can get in your way if you
Follow the highway lines.
Let them drive around you,
Just keep walking in the darkness night.
Defend yourself.

You are all you have,
You are the only one like you.
You can,
You will,
You must,
Defend yourself.
And as you do be at peace.

# CHARLES CITY ROAD

Next morning, they put us in the car, to take a ride.

Years passing,
Daddy beat up everyone.
Until the day we decided to beat him back,
Surprise wake up call.

Whispered,
Jim dear brother and I
Have had enough.
No more fear, no pain,
No anger, no love,
No more.

We must die,
Tonight.

So when he comes through the door
Into our house of horrors,
We hit him,
Hiding behind the door.
Fire poker stick, and
Large glass lamp.
Hitting his head,
Just enough to knock him out.

Cry for help,
Little girl runs,
Walks out into the night.

Police house not far,
A mile to get help.
Brother broke his hand,
Father knocked out on the floor.

Please take me away from here,
Tomorrow, you can live on Charles City Road.

# WITHOUT LIES

They told me and
They told you.

Life can't be lived without lies.

But, I don't believe them.
Do you?

I know what's the truth, and
I'm going to pass it on to you.

Pass it on.
Tell your politicians,
Your neighbors,
And your children, too.

Life.
It can be lived without lies.

The present moment,
A gift to you.

To be the difference maker.
That's right.
Live life to be the difference maker!

Life, it can be lived without lies.

You know people,
Like you and the people like me.
People you can trust to stand beside you!

Truth,
It always comes out in the end.

You just can't buy it down at Wal-Mart.

So, pass it on.
Living life without lies,
White lies, little lies, big lies,
And down-right dirty lies...
About who's been with sleeping with whom?

Oh, Baby,
Tell me the truth.

Do you have any gray hair covered up under that blonde bomb shell?

He left us on Charles City,
that road
Twenty-five years later
returning, the lies.

# DEAR JESUS

What am I going to do?
I cannot sleep,
They tell me you are real, yet everybody's gone.
No mother, no father, no brother,
Dear Jesus,
I have only you.
What am I going to do?
Living now on Charles City Road.

I pray, and I read the words they say are from you.
After I write you this letter,
I look out the window at night and wonder.
How do the stars keep on shinning when the sky is so black?
He drove into the driveway, and said good-bye.

Dear Jesus,
What am I going to do?
I am only a little girl, what did I do?
No mother, no father and now no brother too,
Keep me safe is all that I ask.
And, Jesus replied,
Listen, my voice is softer than a tear,
I am with you always,
You belong to me,
Now, get some rest.

# BE TENDER AND SWEET

Cracked,and Jesus, the Son, seeps into the Wounds
Child of Sorrow and children live all over the World
God's Little Lights of Love
Be Tender and Sweet

Cracked but not Broken
Bruised and Beaten
Shattered
But still Whole
In His Grace

Oh, so Bitter
Feel the stink for a while
See Heaven's Light

Invite Sweetness, Jesus
Tenderness lick the wounds,
Horrible Beatings, little child cries
What a night.

One more drink,
One more fight,
Watching from the eyes of the child,
Hold the door closed, try to keep safe
Child tender and sweet.

Left alone three days in the house
Parents gone.
Where, when, why?
Now I see.
God had a plan before me.

Surrendered, use me now, all grown up
Little and weak, cracked but not broken.
Eating pink and chocolate cupcakes
Hostess without parents for three days,
Just brother and me; Jesus somewhere in the dark.
Will it ever mend? Trusting in You, Jesus.
The test of this life, testing and tired.

But it is in Your tenderness and sweetness
I survived the sea of violence.

# Peace Begins

Create When You Are Broken
One Fostered Child
Truth
Listen When Wisdom Speaks
Be Determined and Strong
Mountain Healing
Forgiveness
Forgiving Mother
Perfect Forgiveness
Mending the Mother's Wound
Washington
Defend Yourself
Echoing Angels
Honor Your Holiness
The Love Song to God
In the Circle of Life
Perfect Timing
Peace Begins

# CREATE WHEN YOU ARE BROKEN

She took out the white paper
and lined up the colored crayons
Which one do I love best?

The blue the red and yellow
I like them all, as she remembered
the new black girl in her class
nobody else was a black, only her.

What can I do with the white crayon
It will not show up on the white paper
and the green crayon is broken,
how can I color with such a little piece?
Create when you are broken.

Green, color me green all over.
It's the color of grass.
it's the color of the trees.
it's the color of money
it's even the color of tea.
How can I color with such a little piece?
Create when you are broken.

I lined all the colors up again
blue, yellow, red, black and green.
And he came in and tore up my paper,
threw the colors all over the room.
He was angry, and I was sad
when he left,
I gathered them all up
And began to create when I was broken.

# ONE FOSTERED CHILD

Who am I? A Kinship – placement
Said one fostered child to another.
But nobody had custody to care.

Reaching out to hold hands as they walked along
A winding, steep, jagged stoned path
Laced with white daisy flowers.

I am a child from the winding whirlwind,
Caught up in a dream catcher's life of lovelessness.

I am a child from the place of wondering.
Wondering why.
My world spins backwards, and
The autumn leaves I see never seem to fall to the ground.

I am a child without the Earth Mother
To support and rock me in the cradle.

A child that only dreams of the provider Father,
And tell me, please,
Who is the Great One supposed to be to me?

Who am I,
Said one fostered child to another?
You are just like me.

Not really so different after all.
Transformed…
Like the lady caterpillar
Slow to break free from the
Wrappings of the tight cocoon.

Transforming night into day, and
Suddenly, just like the fragile butterfly,
Sucking, but not from the Mother's breast.
No, but sipping the nectar of sweetness
From the four-leaf clover.

Gathering life blessings
Singing a new heart song.

Who am I,
Said one fostered child to another,
I am family and friend,
And, then the two of them turned towards the sun
And sat down beside the still waters.

# TRUTH

Truth walks with you wherever you go.

It speaks words of silence,
Sometimes we never hear.

Each petal of your inner, most fragile little self
Becomes stronger in the face of truth.

It is true that the truth will set you free.
It is true that the truth will hurt.

When you can let go of the need
To have your truth be the same for another,
Then truth will shake hands and
Kiss you on each cheek.

In the layers of your truthfulness,
Everyone else exists just
Waiting to come alive
Seeing through the mist.

# LISTEN WHEN WISDOM SPEAKS

Wisdom came to me when I was a child
It said never be afraid.

Wisdom came to me when I was lost
It said never be afraid.

Wisdom came to me when I was sick and tired
It said never be afraid.

Wisdom came to me when I was betrayed
It said never be afraid – to be yourself.

Wisdom came to me when I was learning
It said never be afraid – to fear.

Wisdom came to be when I was poor
It said never be afraid – I am the rich one.

Wisdom came to me and I understood.
Wisdom only comes when I need her the most
and she sings to me the same old song,
The only song that wisdom knows.
And now I know, after all these journeys,
that wisdom knows the truth.
Never be afraid,
And now let wisdom sing to you
never be afraid,
Wisdom's song.

# BE DETERMINED AND STRONG

I read a story once that said
The whirlwind will put you
Right where you belong.

I know that this is true because
That's what happened to me.

Somehow, I made it, because
I was determined and strong.

I was determined to love, when there was no love in sight.
I was strong enough to cry,
When I was dying inside.

In that same story,
It said the people of the village learned to pull together.
Then the whirlwind came along.

And, I think they did so because they were determined and strong.

Being determined means you will get back up,
But, you will not fight.

Being determined means you can bounce back.

Resilience is your power.

Being strong means you know how to bend without breaking.

Resisting nothing

Conquering only yourself.

Being certain that the whirlwind
will put you right where you need to be.

# MOUNTAIN HEALING

The child pleaded, Daddy take me to the mountains
The world has a different and kinder view, and
I want to see
The child pondered, Daddy laughs and sings away his tears
She'll be coming around the mountains
Riding over the hills and turning curves,
The sky is wider and the road takes me to the doors of
Heaven
The long, lonely, hard stretch of road past, the days of
Struggle, grief and all hope is gone
In Mother's abandonment, I cannot play
The mountain peak and valley so low
And Dad says stand beside your brother, Jim
Among the rocks and daisy, he tilts his head
And smiles into the still memory camera scene
The air fills my lungs, and I breathe deep
Mountain Healing
Watching as the memory fills my soul
A motherless two year old, girl child
I stand frozen, grounded into the Mother earth
I am safe and as the breeze sweeps my face
Silent tears of woe and burden my
Heart opens to Mountain Healing
Remembering, God who lives in the mountains
And the Mountain Healing becomes.
A part of the heart magic
And I know we all will go Home soon

# FORGIVENESS

It's time to forgive, cause
Forgiveness and forgetting
Never walk together.

They stand and watch to
See who will win.

Forgiveness, is an act of courage.
It is the essence of what it takes to simply survive.

Forgiveness done correctly
Never allows forgetting to sleep.

Forgiveness is touch love
Wrapped up in see-through paper.

I forgive me.
How about you?

It's time to forgive, family violence ends and peace begins,
hurt, abandoning, abused – abuser – love thru the sin –
cycle stops – don't carry the sword and you win.
If you are a fortunate one in this life
To have someone to forgive,
You are a very lucky indeed.
Cause then, the children sing songs about freedom.

And, if someone blesses you by forgiving you in return,
You are free, so go dance down by the Flowing River,
Hold hands with the child, children everywhere waiting.

Forgiveness is an angel that knows all people everywhere.
It is bread and wine in a crystal gold-trimmed stained glass,
Waiting to be slowly sipped beside still water.

So,
Forgive, cause it is time, to begin peace again.

# FORGIVING MOTHER

Forgiving mother was never easy to do.
I had to do it over and over
And I keep on doing it
Until one day
The forgiving will take place.

She called me up and
Asked me to travel with her on a trip to Florida.

She had been gone a long time...
At least seventeen years.
I never really knew how long.

She was a stranger,
Yet, she was my mother.

So, we traveled together,
Sunny hot days, and
Full moon glowing as we
Drove past the South Carolina border.

Numb from the memories that never existed.
Something happened, and
I forgave her.
I don't remember how it happened.

I didn't think about it, and
She never asked.

We just started picking oranges and laughing.
And, on that one day, I had a mother.
I sat on the crate box, and
She took a picture.

We traveled back, and
I continued my learning,
College, books and blues.

We learned from our mistakes, and
Somewhere in the experience,
I forgave my mother.

# PERFECT FORGIVENESS

Who says forgiving
Makes a difference?

Your mama,
Your papa,
Your church,
Your preacher?

Who says?

Who says forgiving turns your pain into butterflies
Flying to beat the bees for sweet nectar?

Your doctor?
Your next door neighbor that you wish you would have gotten to know?

Who says?

Tell me who told you all the lies about forgiveness?

Forgiveness on the cross,
Forgiveness taught to you as a little child
In some story book sitting in grandma's lap.
Who says forgiveness even matters at all?

I do.
I do, I said.
Did you hear me?
I said,
I do.

As I look into your heart eyes,
Forgiveness makes a difference.

Forgiveness turns around the pain.
Forgiveness taught you as a little child.

So, when it comes time...
And it will...
To forgive you,
I remembered I said,
I do.

I do love you til death do us part,
for better or for worse,
and forgiveness will only work when I let go.

# MENDING THE MOTHER'S WOMB

A journey from womb to wound – and, we will put the pieces
together – Healing the Mother's Wound.
Triumph and trials, a life worth mending – piece by piece. The child turns into a
daughter child – the daughter child into a woman – the woman into a world of the
feminine. The wound heals and the women sing sweet as the world begins to heal.
Mending the Child's Wound – a dedication to the mothers and children
who survive to tell the story – family violence ends, peace begins.

# WASHINGTON

My Daddy took me to Washington.

See there, he said.
Justice becomes your friend, and
Mercy comes from God in the End.

Many walkways, pass driving the bus,
People, and big buildings,
And, along the cracks in the sidewalks,
You see tiny ants,
Crawling to survive.

Washington,
Can you hear the Freedom Bells?

They sleep in that big White House.

The grass never looked greener behind the gate.

See Washington, and the
Sunrise just over the Cherry Blossom Trees.

Sweet Washington singing
Freedom and Justice for All.

Sweet Washington, the neighborhood children
That grew up and broke free.

Justice comes when the rain stops falling,
And the autumn leaves fall down to kiss the Earth.

# DEFEND YOURSELF

You Have A Right
You Deserve The Best
Stand Up And Protect Yourself
If You Don't They Will Take Your Soul
Defend Yourself

Keep Your Stride And Follow
The Lines On The Highway, signs
Do Whatever It Takes To Keep To The
Straight Path
Defend Yourself

Nothing Can Get In Your Way If You
Follow The Highway Lines
Let Them Drive Around You
Just Keep Walking In The Darkness Night
Defend Yourself

You Are All You Have
You Are The Only One Like You
You Can
You Will
You Must
Defend Yourself
And, As You Do Be At Peace.

# ECHOING ANGELS

Echoing angels sing a new song,
Harmony, Peace, and everybody sleeping to a sweet lullaby.

Peace be so still,
In the Silent of the Night.

Echoing Angels,
Beyond this world,
Into the next.

Can't you hear the violins playing,
Comforting tunes,
As the melody makes a new sound and light.

Echoing Angels present only in the twinkle of a star,
Silver glimmers of light.

Behind... a vast night calms you,
Until there is no more storm,
Only Echoing Angels,
Singing a new song.
Harmony, Peace, and everybody is sleeping to a sweet lullaby.

Peace on this Earth,
Declare it so to be,
Now you and me.

Seeing in your neighbors,
Echoing Angels stand.

We together, put down that sword,
We have enough land,
Plant your seeds to grow.

Echoing Angels calling out to the children,
Go, play, and feast upon the sweetness of your living.
Dance to new tunes of simple delight.

Peace, Harmony, and Joy in the stillness of the Night.

# HONOR YOUR HOLINESS

Shaped in the image,
Made by the Creator,
You are Holy.

And, so I am
Spirited by the breath of the great one,
You are Holy.

And, so I am
Because of Love for Soul,
The Great One
Made you to Sing.

And, so I am
Clothed by the perfume art.

Together we are holy.

Timeless One,
Simply sharing a Holy Experience –
Human family circled in love and light.

Honor the Journey,
Become a Traveler
Who remembers.

# THE LOVE SONG TO GOD

Sing me a lullaby,
Play me a soft song and
Caress my neck.

Wipe away the tears with a
Love song to God.

Pour me a glass of milk,
Put my hair in plastic pink curlers.
Cuddle me just after bath.

Who is Aunt Helen?

Hold my hand, tell me a funny story.

Let me look at the pictures of the
Little Blue Boy and Little Pink Girl.

Send me to Sunday School.
Pick me up,
And be a Sunday Driver.

Be my refuge in the storm.
Sing me a Love Song to God.
Sing me a Love song to God.
Sing me a Love song to God.
And, I will remember.

# IN THE CIRCLE OF LIFE

In the circle of life,
We live together,
Heritage, truth, forgiveness,
Sitting in the center of the Play.

# PERFECT TIMING

Timing is all that matters if you're keeping time,
Timing and chance like to race to see if you can
Be there when it matters the most.

Life is time.

Time waits for nobody,
It could be careless if you're not ready or not timing.

Timing rules.
After all, it is the only thing besides love that is eternal.

Love is the ruler of time.
Love sends time out to find you, and
You find each other.

Even if you're not looking at the time that you meet,
It might be a friend, or
It might be a family member.

A lover, or
Anyone you meet on the street.

You don't decide,
Time does.

The right time
Is always now.

Knowing that we can relax and
Wait in between the seconds
of Perfect timing.

# PEACE BEGINS

Peace begins, when family violence ends.
Looking back, you learn the new way
And, you win.
Peace be still my soul.

Peace begins, when family violence ends.
You pray that God will forgive their sins,
And, hold your child hand – innocent.

Peace begins, when family violence ends.
And I sit next to my lost/found kin,
And the scent of Healing Begins.

Peace, give me new roots
sitting next to the trees, nature and me.
Pick the daisy – flower – bouquet
Little Girl within, prunes the family tree,
betrayals and threats forgotten,
smile again.

# About the Author

**CHELSEA ELIZABETH GREEN, MA, LPC** is a licensed professional counselor and has lived in North Carolina for 25 years. North Carolina is home, she loves the mountains and the beaches of North Carolina.

She is the founder and Director of Sage Institute, PLLC, a counseling and Behavioral Health and Wellness training center. Sage offers professional counseling to children and teens recovering from trauma; counseling to families; and organizational team building and consulting to Social Service agencies, businesses and industries that support the health and wellness of their employees. Sage is located in the Garner, NC (Wake County) area and Carthage, NC (Moore County) area.

Chelsea is also a motivational speaker and loves to help others who are dealing with domestic violence. She has 25+ years as a licensed professional counselor in the behavioral health and wellness field. She holds a Master's Degree in Counseling Psychology from Norwich University in Vermont. She has worked as an organizational consultant and trainer for FARR Associates, Inc. and in various other clinical and administrative roles in the mental health and behavioral health and wellness field. She is a member of NC Poets Society.